Art Works™ Drawing fairies and Mermaids

Carolyn Scrace

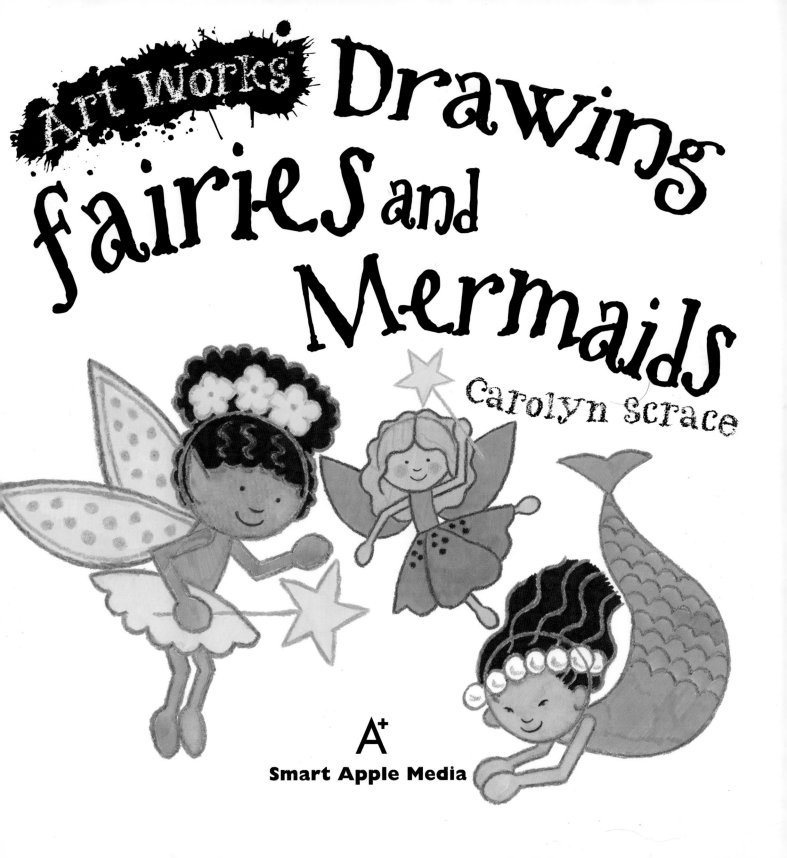

A⁺
Smart Apple Media

Author:
Carolyn Scrace graduated from Brighton College of Art, England, after studying design and illustration. She has since worked in animation, advertising, and children's publishing. She has a special interest in natural history and has written many books on the subject, including *Lion Journal*, and *Gorilla Journal* in the *Animal Journal* series.

How to use this book:

Follow the easy, numbered instructions. Simple step-by-step stages enable budding young artists to create their own amazing drawings.

What you will need:

1. Paper.
2. Wax crayons.
3. Felt-tip pens to add color.

Published by Smart Apple Media,
an imprint of Black Rabbit Books
P.O. Box 3263, Mankato, Minnesota 56002
www.blackrabbitbooks.com

Published by arrangement with
The Salariya Book Company Ltd

Cataloging-in-Publication Data is available from the Library of Congress

Printed in the United States
At Corporate Graphics,
North Mankato, Minnesota

9 8 7 6 5 4 3 2

ISBN: 978-1-62588-345-2

Contents

Fairy Bluebell

1 Fairy Bluebell needs a head,

2 ...a flower-shaped body,

3 ...two legs and feet,

4 ...two arms and hands,

5 ...and two **big** wings!

6 Draw in her hair and two pointed ears!

4

Crayon in spots on Bluebell's wings.

Draw in her eyes, nose, mouth, and rosy cheeks.

Add Bluebell's fairy wand!

Color in with felt-tip pens.

5

Fairy Daisy

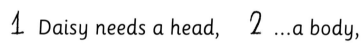 

1 Daisy needs a head, 2 ...a body, 3 ...two legs and feet,

4 ...and two arms and hands. 5 Now draw in her wings and ears! 6 Add a skirt made of **petals**.

Draw in Daisy's bangs with petals around her head!

Add her eyes, nose, and mouth.

Draw in Daisy's fairy wand.

Color in with felt-tip pens.

7

Fairy Poppy

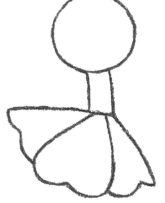

1 Poppy needs a head,

2 ...a body,

3 ...a skirt made from flower petals,

4 ...two legs and feet,

5 ...and two arms, hands, and wings.

6 Now crayon in her long, **wavy** hair.

Add Poppy's
fairy wand!

Draw in her eyes,
nose, mouth, and
two rosy cheeks!

Color in with
felt-tip pens.

9

Fairy Acorn

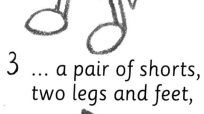

1 Acorn needs a head,

2 ...a **zigzag** body,

3 ... a pair of shorts, two legs and feet,

4 ...two arms and hands,

5 ...and his two wings!

6 Now draw in his pointed ears and acorn-shaped hat!

Add Acorn's fairy wand!

Crayon in a pattern of squares on his acorn-shaped hat.

Draw in his eyes, nose, mouth, and two pink cheeks!

Color in with felt-tip pens.

11

Fairy Buttercup

1 Buttercup needs
a head,

2 ...a body,

3 ...a **frilly** skirt,

4 ...two legs and feet,

5 ...and two arms
and hands.

6 Add two wings
and a pointed ear!

12

Draw in her hair with some flowers.

Add Buttercup's eyes, nose, and mouth.

Draw in her fairy wand.

Color in with felt-tip pens.

13

Fairy Lily

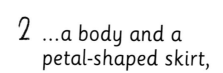

1 Lily needs a head,

2 ...a body and a petal-shaped skirt,

3 ...two legs and feet,

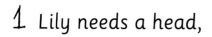

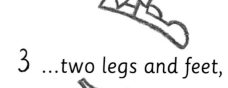

4 ...two arms and hands,

5 ...and two wings.

6 Now draw in a **very big** lily-shaped hat!

14

Draw in Lily's hair.

Draw in her eyes, nose, mouth, and rosy cheeks!

Crayon in spots over her body.

Draw in her fairy wand.

Color in with felt-tip pens.

15

Fairy Leaf

1 Leaf needs a head,

2 ...a body,

3 ...a pair of shorts, two legs, and feet,

4 ...two arms and hands,

5 ...and two wings.

6 Now draw in one ear and add his **curly** hair.

16

Draw in Leaf's eyes, nose, and mouth.

Draw in his fairy wand.

Add crayon lines to make his wings look like leaves.

Color in with felt-tip pens.

17

Mermaid Shelly

Tail fin

1 Shelly needs
a head,

2 ...a body and a
tail fin,

3 ...two arms
and hands,

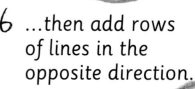

4 ... and **very
long**, curly hair.

5 To make the fish-scale
pattern: draw lines in
one direction,

6 ...then add rows
of lines in the
opposite direction.

Crayon in tiny shells
to decorate her hair.

Draw in Shelly's eyes,
nose, mouth, and two
rosy cheeks!

Color in with
felt-tip pens.

Mermaid Pearl

Tail fin →

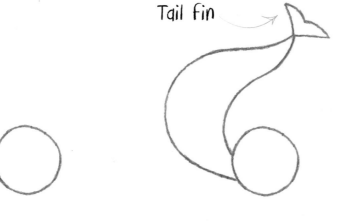

1 Pearl needs a head,

2 ...a body and a tail fin,

3 ...two arms and hands,

4 ...two ears and a **pearl** headband,

5 ...and long curly hair.

6 Draw in the wavy pattern of her scales.

Color in with felt-tip pens.

Draw in Pearl's eyes, nose, and mouth.

21

Mermaid Star

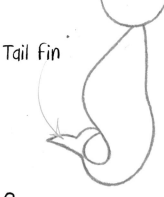

Tail fin

1 Star needs a head,

2 ...a body and a tail fin,

3 ...two arms and hands,

4 ...long, flowing hair,

5 ...a **star** in her hair and a matching pendant.

6 Now draw the pattern of her scales!

Draw in Star's
eyes, nose,
and mouth.

Color in with
felt-tip pens.

23

Mermaid Coral

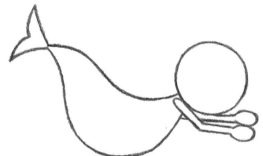

1 Coral needs a head,

2 ...a body and a tail fin,

Tail fin

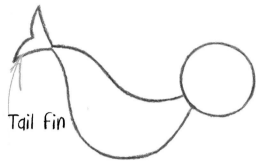

3 ...two arms and hands,

4 ...two ears and **very curly** hair.

5 To make a fish-scale pattern: draw lines in one direction,

6 ...then add rows of lines in the opposite direction.

Draw in Coral's
eyes, nose, and
mouth.

Add some shells and
a starfish to decorate
her hair.

Color in with
felt-tip pens.

25

Mermaid Marina

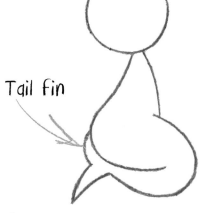

Tail fin

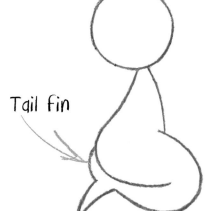

1 Marina needs a head,

2 ...a body and a tail fin,

3 ...two arms and hands,

4 ...two ears and long, wavy hair.

5 Draw in the fish-scale pattern.

6 Add her eyes, nose, and mouth.

Crayon in some
**pretty
seaweed**
on Marina's hair.

Color in with
felt-tip pens.

27

Mermaid Breeze

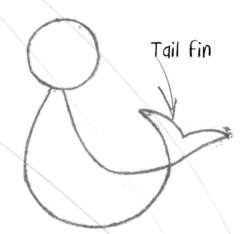

Tail fin

1 Breeze needs a head,

2 ...a body and a tail fin,

3 ...two arms and hands,

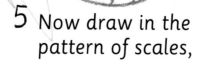

4 ...one ear and curly hair.

5 Now draw in the pattern of scales,

6 ...and her eyes, nose, and mouth.

Crayon in a
starfish
on her hair.

Draw in Breeze's
shell trumpet!

Color in with
felt-tip pens.

29

Mermaid Misty

Tail fin

1 Misty needs a head,

2 ...a body, and a tail fin,

3 ...and two ears, two arms and hands!

4 Now draw five seashells around the top of her head,

5 ...and add long **flowing** hair.

6 Crayon in the pattern of her scales.

Crayon in spots on Misty's tail fin.

Color in with felt-tip pens.

Draw in Misty's eyes, nose, and mouth.

31

Glossary

Acorn a smooth nut in a cup-shaped holder, the fruit of an oak tree.

Fairy a tiny imaginary being in human form, with magical powers.

Mermaid an imaginary sea creature, half woman, and half fish.

Pattern a repeated shape or design used to decorate something.

Pearl a smooth, round jewel formed inside an oyster or clam shell.

Scale a flat plate forming part of the body-covering of fish and other animals.

Seaweed a plant that grows in the sea. You will often find it washed up on beaches.

Starfish a sea creature, usually with five arms, that feeds on shellfish.

Tail fin a fin at the rear end of a fish, whale, etc.

Index